The mere chink of cups and saucers
tunes the mind to happy repose.
Anon

TEA

&

CONVERSATION

Develop the art of conversation
with afternoon tea

Copper Beech Publishing

Published in Great Britain by
Copper Beech Publishing Ltd
© Beryl Peters/Copper Beech Publishing Ltd 2000

ISBN 978-1-898617-25-9

A CIP catalogue record for this book is available from
The British Library

Copper Beech Publishing Ltd
P O Box 159, East Grinstead,
Sussex RH19 4FS England

*Scarcely any thing is so repulsive in a lady
— so utterly plebeian - as speaking in
a loud harsh voice. As in Shakespeare's time,
a "soft, gentle and low" voice is still considered
"an excellent thing in woman."*

INTRODUCTION

Tea and conversation are natural soulmates. They belong together, entwined as good companions from times gone by. Their combination, with the accompanying traditions, goes back through eras that relied on social graces to form the structure of society.

But it is not only British history that is steeped in the tea traditions. Such countries as Japan and China celebrated tea drinking, stressing the importance of hospitality. The legends of tea discovery are diverse and fascinating and make a good read, but in the early days there was one common fact - tea was drunk for its beneficial properties which encouraged a feeling of well-being, relaxation - and conversation. In short, it was a social thing.

To listen well is as powerful a means of influence as to talk well, and is essential to all true conversation.

It is no coincidence, then, that our 'Penny Universities', the common name given to coffee houses as early as the 1650s, were so popular. In them, the new and exotic tastes of tea, coffee and cocoa were introduced to customers who were welcome to continue their business conversations in the warm havens they provided. Tea and convivial surroundings encouraged open debate, lengthy discussions and social gossip.

Women, however, were not allowed the freedom of the coffee houses. Those who could afford the luxury of tea had to send a servant to the apothecary to buy and infuse it at home. And, to safeguard against theft, the mistress often took charge of the locked tea-caddy, presiding over the whole process and sometimes even washing the small, delicate china bowls in which tea was served.

Hospitality is a wonderful thing. It warms the heart and sharpens the wits by the interchange of ideas.

Making tea was time-consuming, so the habit of inviting friends to join in was established. Anna, the 7th Duchess of Bedford, was largely responsible for setting this fashion and it was followed by the rich and middle classes alike. These women were often at a loss for ways of entertaining themselves, as much was still forbidden them. Needless to say, the concept of 'afternoon tea' was eagerly accepted and perfected!

Much has changed since the formal settings of tea drinking in those early days. Nowadays we may be more relaxed about our tea drinking but we still relish these enjoyable periods of relaxation. When tea flows, so does conversation and, although we may not realise it, we are continuing an age-old custom from a time when life was more leisurely and afternoons seemed longer.

The art of conversation consists as much in listening politely, as in talking agreeably.

Atwell

HOW TO RECEIVE GUESTS FOR AFTERNOON TEA

*There is no conversation so graceful, so varied,
so sparkling, as that of an intellectual and
cultivated woman.*

When receiving guests, your first object should be to make them feel at home; whether you are a mistress of a mansion or a cottage the rules are the same. You must endeavour to make their visit agreeable. Let your friends be assured from your manner, that their presence is a real enjoyment to you.

As the hostess it is your duty to see that your guests are comfortably seated at table and their wants attended to. When it comes to conversation, all of them have the same claims to your attention.

*Even when positive as to the correctness of your view of
a subject in which you may differ in opinion from any of
the company, though you may assert it firmly and
gently, avoid every thing like pedantry or dogmatism.
Such a display in a lady is always repulsive ...*

OUT TO TEA

Time for intimate conversation ...

Many ladies prefer to be seen out and about, visiting quaint little tea shops. These provide the perfect meeting place with a good cup of tea, the company of friends, all in comforts similar to home. What a wonderful setting to chatter about the latest fashions!

In London town, a favourite meeting place is Gunter's of Berkeley Square. This and the other well-known hotel tea rooms offer a place to be seen after the bustle of shopping.

Nowadays the motor car widens our horizons and an afternoon outing, with time for intimate conversation while travelling, is a special treat. The company of a friend, a pot of tea and fresh made cake in a village tea-shop is most enjoyable.

TEA & CONVERSATION
THROUGHOUT THE YEAR

A good hostess will make her choice of food according to the season and the degree of formality.

Afternoon tea is the ideal time to meet friends and each season brings with it its own topics for conversation.

The hostess should be as adventurous in her choice of food, table decoration and conversation as in her choice of dress, all with the aim of impressing the visitor.

She must match the colour of the tablecloth and napkins to the month of the year. She should also follow the colour scheme with the food. The colour of sandwich fillings should be carefully chosen, crêpe paper frills placed around dainty morsels, icings colour coded and the jellies, desserts, garnishes and relishes should all blend in!

Guests will be delighted to receive dainty sandwiches with various fillings such as cucumber, anchovy paste, egg and cress - and finely cut ham.

Thin slices of seeded home-baked bread, spread with butter and home-made preserves, will also please guests. Scones, cakes, buns, muffins, gingerbreads and biscuits could be on offer too, together with fresh fruits or sorbets.

The drawing room tea is not meant to be a filling meal for hungry people, but a dainty snack to accompany tea drinking. It bridges the gap between lunch and dinner, which has steadily become later and later in the evening.

Guests should not be pressed to take more than they have inclination for. This would be both antiquated and rude of the hostess.

As empty vessels make the loudest sound, so they that have least wit are the greatest babblers.
Plato

Nowhere is there room for the display of good manners so much as in conversation. It is a part of good manners not to talk too much.

One of the greatest pleasures in life is conversation.
Sydney Smith

TEA & CONVERSATION IN SPRINGTIME

In order to talk well, three conditions are indisputable,
- tact, a good memory and a fair education.

Springtime offers great scope for the enthusiastic hostess. The isolation of winter months ensures plenty of guests, an eagerness for new conversation and the latest styles.

For those who have wintered abroad, afternoon tea is the perfect showcase for their European fashions and for those who have spent cosy days at home dressmaking, the fruits of their work could be paraded.

The awakening of the flowerbeds will inspire the astute hostess in spring and Easter. She will plan her afternoon tea to be at one with the countryside, to echo nature all around her.

Yellows, greens and violets are the most popular colours for this season. The hostess will collect garden and wild flowers to adorn her table; she will make a vivid table decoration to be a visual masterpiece which will stimulate conversation, and put guests at their ease.

The hostess must remember to regulate the height of any centrepiece so that guests are not straining to glimpse and converse with each other through the foliage!

A theme should be chosen and the table cloth, napkins, tea equipage, china, doilies, table runners and all trimmings will be coordinated in accordance with the theme. The cloth might be embroidered with crocus and tulips and the corner of the napkins decorated with matching imagery. Where possible the crockery should match one of the colours, as would the tray cloth.

... the happiest conversation ...
where there is no competition, no vanity, but a calm
quiet interchange of ideas.
Samuel Johnson

ADVICE FOR YOUNG MEN'S CONVERSATION AT TEA PARTIES

These first teas of the spring season were the ideal time to introduce young men into adult gatherings. They needed to practise the art of conversation before being launched into the male world of commerce.

Bumptiousness, loudness, selfishness and swagger are unattractive, while undue or marked deference to rank or age is ill-bred.

Young men should try to engage the conversation of those women who are not the most lavishly supplied with personal beauty. Such persons have cultivated their manners and conversation more than those who can rely upon their natural endowments. The absence of pride and pretension will have improved their good nature and they are not too much occupied in contemplating their own charms, to be not disposed to indulge in gentle criticism of others.

ADVICE FOR YOUNG MEN'S CONVERSATION AT TEA PARTIES

The finest compliment that can be paid to a woman of refinement and esprit is to lead the conversation into such a channel as may mark your appreciation of her superior attainments. Let your conversation be adapted as skilfully as may be to your company.

Never lower the intellectual standard of your conversation in addressing ladies. Pay them the compliment of seeming to consider them capable of an equal understanding with gentlemen.

Do not use a classical quotation without apologising for or translating it. Whether in the presence of ladies or gentlemen, much display of learning is out of place.

The tone of good conversation is brilliant and natural.
It is neither tedious nor frivolous.
Jean-Jacques Rousseau

Recipe on a Spring Green Theme
Green Butter Sandwiches

2oz fresh butter
2oz boned anchovies
3oz parsley or spinach
Thin slices of bread or thin olive biscuits

Pound the butter and anchovies to a thin paste together. Chop the parsley or spinach as fine as possible, then dry them with a cloth. Mix well with the paste. Spread two slices of bread rather thickly and lay on top another slice. Press firmly together.

If we are to improve our minds by conversation it is a great happiness to be acquainted with persons older than ourselves.

*Good talk is like good scenery – continuous, yet
constantly varying, and full of the charm of
novelty and surprise.*
Randolph S. Bourne

26

TEA & CONVERSATION IN THE SUMMER

*In our pleasant chats at afternoon teas and
tennis-parties we can well dispense with stilted talk.
Conversation now is more simple and natural,
less dogmatic and egoistical.*

The freedom of the outside setting can lead guests to forget the rules of conversation. Although the relaxed atmosphere is encouraged it should be remembered that the first syllable of conversation is 'con' (with), - that it means talking with another person. We should abstain from lecturing and always be as ready to listen as to talk!

The art of conversation for both inside and outside is the duty of a woman to cultivate. She should be acquainted with the current news and historical events of at least the last few years and carefully introduce a topic when the chatter is becoming too frivolous.

When talking, the voice should be gentle and low. Slang and puns are vulgar too and in no way a substitute for wit. During the summer months it is easy to let standards of conversation slip. Some women think that to adopt the saucy chic of Americanisms is amusing.

A loud voice is both disagreeable and vulgar –
even in the garden.

An abundance of vibrant colours opens all kinds of possibilities for a summer afternoon tea party and the chance of entertaining guests in the garden offers a different dimension. Of course, the wise hostess will always have a contingency plan ready in case of inclement weather! As to the colour scheme, one is spoilt for choice but the reds of roses and poppies offer dramatic contrasts to white table linen.

A pretty arbour, a lawn shaded by overhanging tree branches, or a flat patch near the garden stream all make ideal settings for an outside tea.

Unlike the picnic, where guests expect to lounge on rugs for *al fresco* refreshments, afternoon tea guests will expect to be seated. The tea table should be presented almost as if tea was to be taken indoors.

In deciding on flowers for the table, the colouring of the china must be taken into account. A very pretty idea for the centre of the table is the miniature lake composed of a flat, oval, or round mirror, bordered with moss or fern fronds, amongst which may nestle clusters of any small flowers, their beauty reflected on the clear surface of the glass. This would be especially attractive for the table set beside the stream.

The hostess must be careful when introducing any anecdotes in to the conversation to keep them short, witty, eloquent, and not too far-fetched as the sun often tires the guests, reducing their attention span.

The first ingredient in conversation is truth; the next, good sense; the third, good humour and the fourth, wit.
Sir William Temple

A Simple Tea-cake Recipe 1896

Take one large tablespoonful of butter and beat to a cream, with one cup and a half of white sugar. Add the beaten yolks of two eggs and one cup of milk. Then stir in two cups of flour mixed with two teaspoons of baking powder. Beat till smooth, and then add the beaten egg whites and flavouring, say, two scant teaspoons. Raisins, currants or citron may be added and give a pleasant flavour. Bake in small pans for twenty minutes in a moderate oven. These may be iced if liked. This recipe makes a dozen fair-sized cakes.

Remember – a word of kindness is seldom spoken in vain, while witty sayings are as easily lost as the pearls slipping from a broken string.
G.D. Prentice

AN ARBOUR IS ALWAYS POPULAR—IF IT BE
FRESH AND CLEAN SWEPT AND FREE FROM
WEEDS, DAMP, AND DECAY.

*Drawn by
P. Clarke.*

The mere chink of cups and saucers tunes
the mind to happy repose.
Anon

TEA & CONVERSATION IN THE AUTUMN

*Great talent for conversation should be accompanied
by great politeness.*

After a long summer, women are eager to discard their flimsier dresses and bring out their heavier more ornate fashions. The outside chill and autumnal shades beckon guests to the drawing room where the closeness of the walls draws intimate conversation.

The afternoon tea in autumn is the ideal opportunity for the eager hostess to try her hand at a formal tea party. This will refresh her mind for the successions of dinner parties to come.

For this more formal afternoon tea, notes of invitation or acceptance are written in the third person and the simplest style. They should be written on paper of the best quality and be enclosed in envelopes.

Invitations are issued in the name of the mistress of the house only and can follow the form:

Mrs Jones requests the pleasure of
Mrs Thomson's company
on Tuesday 15th May
at 4 o'clock for afternoon tea.

The reply should be as follows:

Mrs Thomson has much pleasure
in accepting Mrs Jones' kind invitation
for afternoon tea
on Tuesday at 4 o'clock.

Draw up a menu of conversation –

As the hostess took so long attending to the table decorations, the food, the choice of guests and her appearance, she should also be aware of shaping the conversation.

So that the guests would quickly be in touch with each other, the hostess could also scheme the talk by drawing up menus of conversation; these could be placed on each person's plate.

At a formal tea party it is wrong to consider the art of conversation unimportant. It is one's duty to try to make others happy.

"It has always seemed absurd to me to be so careful about what we put into our mouths, and to leave to chance to arrange what comes out of them."

"Silence propagates itself, and the longer talk has been suspended, the more difficult it is to find something to say."
Samuel Johnson

We English with our reserved temperament and aloof attitude, often regard conversation as a frivolous occupation and some say we make better company with a set menu for conversation.

The conversation menu would suggest two or three different topics on each list and these could be subtly introduced when there is a lull in conversation. The skills of conversation should be used artfully so that no one realises that your topic of conversation has been taken from the list!

The weather has so often given serviceable help in breaking the blank pause that ensues upon our introduction to a stranger at the tea table.

It is one of the most difficult things properly to arrange guests, and to place them in such a manner that the conversation may always be general.

Gingerbread for tea

The homely luxury, gingerbread, has been popular ever since the fourteenth century. In those days, it was made and sold in Paris, prepared with rye-meal made into a dough; ginger, other spices, sugar and honey were kneaded into it.

It was introduced in to England by the court of Henry the Fourth for their festivals, and was soon brought into general use, treacle being after a time employed in the manufacture instead of honey.

'There is an increasing amount of conversation at table these days devoted to the subject of diet and fat.'
A few words on conversation 1893

Recipe for Scotch Gingerbread 1893

½lb groats	¼lb plain flour
2oz margarine	2oz lard
10oz sultanas	6oz treacle

¼ teaspoon ground ginger
¼ teaspoon ground cinnamon
¼ gill milk (2 tablespoons)
¼ teaspoon bicarbonate soda
2oz brown moist sugar

Mix together the groats, flour, spices and fruit.
Melt together the fat, treacle and sugar. Stir into dry
ingredients and finally add the soda melted in the
milk. Bake in a moderate oven for 45-60 minutes.

Silence is one great art of conversation. **Hazlitt**

"Conversation should be pleasant, without scurrility, witty without affection, audacious without impudency, learned without opinion, and strange without heresy."

Love's Labour's Lost
William Shakespeare

TEA & CONVERSATION IN THE WINTER

*Never let your conversation merely be an
exercising of the tongue.*

The winter afternoon tea can take on an air
of informality. In this way, the hostess is not
greatly inconvenienced if the adverse weather
stops her guests from making the journey at the last
minute. It also allows people to stay less time if
they are overburdened with preparations for their
own dinner guests, as is often the case during the
long winter evenings.

On this informal occasion, tea could be
served around the fire, in a cosy manner, with the
drawing room drapes closed against the winter
cold.

The tea table should be laden with crockery,
food and tea. It can be decorated with a suitable
arrangement of winter flowers and foliage – perhaps holly.

The guests should sit wherever they feel at ease, absorbing the warmth from the open fire, talking together whilst enjoying their afternoon tea.

A less formal invitation could take the form of a friendly note, something in this manner:

> *Dear Miss Sanderson,*
> *We have some friends coming to drink tea with us to-morrow. Will you give us the pleasure of your company also?*
> *We hope you will not disappoint us.*

This is the ideal occasion to introduce younger ladies to afternoon tea - and of course to the art of making refined conversation. So that they are usefully employed, they can pass around the plates of food and replenish empty teacups.

This ensures that they are not left sitting in a corner at this difficult age between them being too old for nursery tea yet too young for all adult gatherings.

*One should **always** say
"drink tea" and not "take tea"
which is a vulgarism!*

Not all young girls are gifted with charming manners. Some are painfully shy and others are precocious and argumentative! Timidity is common when first introduced into an adult gathering.

If a young gentleman is present the young girl should be natural in her conversation, neither prim nor giggling and flirtatious. Knowledge of world affairs will not be at her disposal for conversation. She is absorbed in her home circle, her pets and her sports. Such a girl may be a delightful companion as long as she is taught that her stories must not be too long-winded.

She should cultivate the art of silence until included in the conversation, as listening is a good way of learning. A loud voice, loud laughter and flashy manner will bring disapproval. A deference to convention is expected of her.

"Now for the banquet we press;
  Now for the eggs, the ham,
  Now for the mustard and cress,
  Now for the strawberry jam!
  Now for the tea of our host,
  Now for the rollicking bun,
  Now for the muffin and toast,
  Now for the gay Sally Lunn!"

The Sorcerer 1877 **W S** Gilbert

Younger ladies could take charge of the 'toasting tray', being accustomed to this in the nursery.

Next to the open fire, loaded with slices of bread, muffins, butter, conserves and the all-important toasting fork, it can keep them busy and provide a source of fun and conversation!

They will delight in serving a few guests with their toasted choice, straight from the heat of the fire and drizzled with butter.

SILENCE ...

Long silences can be very embarrassing, but never talk for the mere sake of talking! Nothing is so repulsive as the never-ceasing voice of people who deem it a virtue rather to give utterance to foolishness than to be altogether silent.

༼ᴐ

He has occasional flashes of silence, that make his conversations perfectly delightful.
Sydney Smith

༼ᴐ

That silence is one of the great arts of conversation is allowed by Cicero himself, who says that there is not only an art, but an eloquence in it.
Hannah More

༼ᴐ

He speaks not; and yet there lies
A conversation in his eyes.
Longfellow

SILENCE ...

The experienced hostess has usually at hand a few light subjects and ideas to fill those awkward moments:-

"In dinner talk it is better, perhaps allowable, to fling any faggot rather than let the fire go out."
J.M.Barrie

No interruptions please!
"There cannot be a greater rudeness than to interrupt
another in the current of his discourse."
John Locke

GOSSIP ...

*Remember - scandal is the least excusable of all
conversational vulgarities.*

There is gossip and there is gossip. The word
gossip has fallen into disrepute; it is associated with
slander, trivial carpings, and criticisms of others. This
type of gossip should never be used. Gossip which is
hurtful and cynical can be amusing enough; it can
make you laugh against your will, but it leaves a bad
taste in your mouth.

However, some women make excellent hostesses
simply because they are charming gossips. They use
their art to mirror a genuine liking for, and interest in,
their fellow-creatures and their harmless eccentrici-
ties and innocent foibles.

SUBJECTS TO AVOID IN CONVERSATION

You may talk of all subjects but one - namely
your maladies.
Ralph Waldo Emerson

In searching for the elements of conversation, never have recourse to abstruse or little-understood subjects. If you comprehend them fully yourself, every one will suppose that you have chosen them for the sake of display – if you do not, your confusion of ideas will speedily expose you to the contempt of your auditors.

"There is one subject peremptorily forbidden to all
rational mortals, namely, their distempers. If you have
not slept, or if you have slept, or if you have a headache,
or sciatica, or leprosy or thunder-stroke, I beseech you,
by all angels, to hold your peace, and not pollute the
morning by corruption and groans."
Ralph Waldo Emerson

SUBJECTS TO AVOID IN CONVERSATION

... generally indulged in by persons devoid of brains,
education and culture ...

It is far safer to avoid personalities in conversation. Having an over interest in our neighbours' affairs makes it difficult to prevent gossip. This kind of personal talk is generally indulged in by persons devoid of brains, education and culture. People who read and think, prefer to talk of ideas and things. Chit-chat about neighbours' income, quarrels and dress are wearisome.

Never boast either openly or indirectly. Do not monopolise all the conversation. Avoid disgraceful and uncalled for criticism. Do not tell over long stories about yourself. It is wrong to boast of your own exploits. Do not indulge in slang.

51

SUBJECTS TO AVOID IN CONVERSATION

"My child said such a witty thing last night ..."

Make not thy own person, family, relations, or affairs the frequent subject of thy tattle.

Say not:

> *"My manner and custom is to do this ..."*
> *"I neither eat nor drink in the morning ..."*
> *"I am apt to be troubled with corns ..."*
> *"My child said such a witty thing last night ..."*
> Fuller

GOOD HUMOUR IN CONVERSATION ...

A good laugh is sunshine in a house. Thackeray

✎

Conversation never sits easier than when we now and then discharge ourselves in a symphony of laughter; which may not improperly be called the chorus of conversation. Steele

✎

Good humour may be said to be one of the very best articles of dress one can wear in society.   Thackeray

✎

A laugh is worth a hundred groans in any market.
Lamb

✎

Laughter is a most helpful exertion; it is one of the greatest helps to digestion which I am acquainted; and the custom prevalent amongst our forefathers, of exciting it at table by jesters and buffoons, was founded on true medical principles. Hufeland

*In conversation, humour is more than wit and easiness
more than knowledge. Few desire to learn, or think
they need it – All desire to be pleased, or at least to be
easy.* **Sir William Temple**

OFTEN ASKED QUESTIONS OF ETIQUETTE
1890-1899

What is the correct way of dispensing afternoon tea?
Mother

You ought to pour it out and hand it to the guests yourself; if however, you have any young girls in the family, they should relieve you of the latter duty.

Is it correct to use a tray cloth on a silver tea tray?

It is not usual to have a tray cloth on a silver tray, as this detracts so from the effect. You could use small cork mats under the pots. Old and priceless silver is often a trifle marked but this just adds to its interest in showing the length of time it has been in use.

In conversation are interruptions permitted?

Be cautious at all times not to interrupt others. It is a solecism for the frequent recurrence of which no brilliancy of remark can atone.

OFTEN ASKED QUESTIONS OF ETIQUETTE
1890–1899

Should men wear knickerbockers in the drawing-room at afternoon tea?

Certainly; tea-time is an informal meal in the country, and a man wears his ordinary "work-a-day" dress until dinner time.

Should a five o'clock tea-table be set before or after the guests arrive?

Either is correct. If the room is small and many guests are arriving, it is often more convenient to the servant to have brought in the tea-table, tray, tea-service and whatever else is needed, only adding the tea, hot water, and hot cakes at the proper tea time.

When a visitor calls should I have cups of tea handed round, or pour it out myself?

It is more graceful and at the same time correct to pour tea out yourself; the essence of hospitality consists in taking people into your home life.

OFTEN ASKED QUESTIONS OF ETIQUETTE
1890-1899

In conversation, how frequently should I repeat the title of the person addressed?

Repeating a title too frequently savours of meanness and servility. Waiting-women may be allowed to garnish their talk with an oft-repeated "my lady," but in conversation a lady will use this epithet sparingly. An occasional " Your ladyship," just to show that you recognise and respect her rank, is all that the dictates of good taste allow – is indeed all that is required.

What should one do with a guest who is a bore ...?

Everyone knows from painful experience what is meant by a bore! A bore is a heavy, pompous meddling person who harps on one string, occupies an undue share of conversation, and says things in ten words which required only two; do not repeat the invitation!

CONVERSATIONAL WISDOM

Speaking without thinking is shooting without aiming.
W.G. Benham

༭

*Talk often, but never long: in that case, if you do not
please, at least you are sure not to tire your hearers.*
Lord Chesterfield

༭

So much they talked, so very little said.
Charles Churchill

༭

Many can argue, not many converse.
Amos Bronson Alcott

༭

*I have always had a great respect for a Philippine
proverb; "Into the closed mouth the fly does not get."*
Theodore Roosevelt, Jr.

IS CONVERSATION A DYING ART ... ? 1895

It is probably inevitable that the excessive nervous tension and the high speed of our present life is bound to have a deteriorating effect on all branches of art, but it seems a pity that more effort is not being made to recapture the lost art of conversation. There is no time to read intellectual books. The modern reader asks for a book easily read, with a thrilling plot and a happy ending.

Bridge is a killer of conversation. How can you expect brilliancy of thought or speech from anyone who has sat for hours at a game of bridge?

Younger people sigh for dancing, elder ones for a game of bridge and after commenting on the weather, discussing the latest scandal, and the doings of several absent friends - all topics are found to be exhausted around the tea table. The bored guests make their way home early!

Most important of all a woman's accomplishments is the ability to maintain an intelligent, vivacious conversation with family, friends and guests. A woman who is a good talker and can talk equally well whatever may be the character of her guests, is a blessing to the world.
An Important Accomplishment 1885

THE ETIQUETTE COLLECTION *Collect the set!*
ETIQUETTE FOR COFFEE LOVERS
Fresh coffee - the best welcome in the world!
Enjoy the story of coffee drinking,
coffee etiquette and recipes.

ETIQUETTE FOR CHOCOLATE LOVERS
Temptation through the years.
A special treat for all Chocolate Lovers.

THE ETIQUETTE OF NAMING THE BABY
'A good name keeps its lustre in the dark.'
Old English Proverb

THE ETIQUETTE OF AN ENGLISH TEA
How to serve a perfect English afternoon tea;
traditions, superstitions, recipes and how to read your
fortune in the tea-leaves afterwards.

THE ETIQUETTE OF ENGLISH PUDDINGS
Traditional recipes for good old-fashioned
puddings - together with etiquette notes
for serving.

ETIQUETTE FOR GENTLEMEN
*'If you have occasion to use your handkerchief
do so as noiselessly as possible.'*